Fanciful Fox
Mosaic Adult Color By Number Book
Adult Coloring Book for Stress Relief and Relaxation

By Color Questopia

Thank you
for your purchase!

**Claim your FREE digital copy of our
Highlight Reel Color By Number Book:**

Check out our website: colorquestopia.com

**Join our Facebook group:
facebook.com/colorquestopia**

Follow us on Instagram: @colorquestopia

**Did you enjoy this book?
Please leave us a review!**

https://geni.us/cqreview

Color By Number Tips

1. **Relax and have fun**
   Let your cares slip away as you color the images. Take your time. Coloring is a meditative activity and there's no wrong way to do it. Feel free to color as you listen to music, watch TV, lounge in bed- do whatever relaxes you most! You can also color while you're out and about- on the train or at a cafe- take the book with you anywhere you go. Coloring is therapeutic and is great for stress relief and relaxation!

2. **Colors corresponding to each number are shown on the back cover of the book**
   Each number corresponds to a color shown on the back of the book. You can match the color as closely as you like- but feel free to change the color or the shade if you don't have the exact color match- that's totally fine. Although this is a color by number book, it's completely okay to get creative and color the images with whichever colors you like and have. The numbers are there to be a guide and to allow you to color without having to focus your energy on choosing colors.

3. **Choose your coloring tools**
   Everyone has their favorite coloring markers, crayons, pencils, pens- even paints! Feel free to color with any tool that you like! If you choose markers or paints, we recommend putting a blank sheet of paper or cardboard behind each image, so that your colors don't run onto the next image.

Enjoy!

1. Black

2. Dark Brown

3. Medium Orange

4. Yellow

5. Medium Yellow

6. Medium Brown

7. Light Gray

8. Light Brown

9. Brown

10. Dark Orange

11. Orange

12. Light Orange

13. Dark Green

14. Light Green

15. Neon Green

16. Gray

17. Sky Blue

1. Dark Brown

2. Medium Brown

3. Orange

4. Medium Brown

5. Light Brown

6. Medium Orange

7. Brown

8. Dark Yellow

9. Dark Orange

10. Dark Gray

11. Gray

12. Medium Gray

13. Light Gray

14. Green

15. Light Green

16. Blue

17. Sky Blue

1. Black

2. Dark Brown

3. Light Yellow

4. Light Orange

5. Light Brown

6. Medium Brown

7. Brown

8. Yellow

9. Green

10. Light Green

11. Dark Green

12. Dark Gray

13. Medium Gray

14. Gray

15. Light Gray

16. Sky Blue

17. Blue

1. Black

2. Dark Brown

3. Light Red

4. Yellow

5. Medium Yellow

6. Medium Orange

7. Light Yellow

8. Brown

9. Light Orange

10. Orange

11. Light Brown

12. Dark Yellow

13. Dark Gray

14. Light Gray

15. Green

16. Light Green

17. Sky Blue

18. Blue

1. Dark Brown

2. Light Red

3. Dark Orange

4. Yellow

5. Light Yellow

6. Light Orange

7. Medium Brown

8. Light Brown

9. Brown

10. Army Green

11. Dark Green

12. Light Green

13. Neon Green

14. Medium Green

15. Green

16. Light Blue

17. Medium Blue

1. Black

2. White

3. Dark Brown

4. Light Yellow

5. Light Orange

6. Yellow

7. Dark Red

8. Light Red

9. Light Red

10. Light Gray

11. Gray

12. Light Brown

13. Green

14. Light Green

15. Dark Green

16. Light Blue

17. Blue

1. Black

2. Dark Brown

3. Light Yellow

4. Yellow

5. Light Orange

6. Dark Orange

7. Medium Orange

8. Dark Yellow

9. Dark Gray

10. Brown

11. Light Brown

12. Medium Brown

13. Red

14. Green

15. Dark Green

16. Light Green

17. Dark Red

1. Black

2. Dark Brown

3. Light Yellow

4. Yellow

5. Orange

6. Medium Brown

7. Light Brown

8. Dark Yellow

9. Brown

10. Neon Green

11. Army Green

12. Medium Green

13. Green

14. Dark Green

15. Light Green

16. Sky Blue

17. Blue

1. Black
2. Dark Brown
3. Orange
4. Light Orange
5. Light Yellow
6. Yellow
7. Medium Orange
8. Medium Yellow
9. Medium Brown
10. Light Gray
11. Dark Yellow
12. Light Brown
13. Green
14. Light Green
15. Dark Green
16. Blue
17. Sky Blue

1. Black

2. Dark Brown

3. Light Red

4. Orange

5. Light Orange

6. Light Brown

7. Light Yellow

8. Medium Orange

9. Brown

10. Green

11. Dark Green

12. Medium Orange

13. Light Green

14. Dark Green

15. Neon Green

16. Blue

17. Light Blue

1. Black

2. Dark Brown

3. Light Pink

4. Light Orange

5. Light Yellow

6. Yellow

7. Medium Yellow

8. Medium Orange

9. Light Brown

10. Brown

11. Dark Brown

12. Dark Orange

13. Green

14. Dark Green

15. Dark Gray

16. Gray

17. Sky Blue

1. Black

2. Dark Brown

3. Light Red

4. Yellow

5. Light Orange

6. Light Yellow

7. Dark Yellow

8. Light Brown

9. Medium Orange

10. Medium Brown

11. Orange

12. Beige

13. Brown

14. Army Green

15. Dark Gray

16. Light Gray

17. Green

18. Light Blue

1. Black

2. Dark Brown

3. Light Orange

4. Light Yellow

5. Light Brown

6. Yellow

7. Beige

8. Dark Yellow

9. Brown

10. Medium Brown

11. Dark Green

12. Army Green

13. Green

14. Light Green

15. Light Blue

16. Medium Blue

17. Dark Blue

1. Black

2. Dark Brown

3. Light Orange

4. Beige

5. Light Brown

6. Orange

7. Medium Brown

8. Brown

9. Light Gray

10. Gray

11. Army Green

12. Light Green

13. Dark Green

14. Green

15. Medium Green

16. Neon Green

17. Light Blue

1. Black

2. Dark Brown

3. Light Orange

4. Light Yellow

5. Light Brown

6. Orange

7. Beige

8. Dark Yellow

9. Medium Brown

10. Brown

11. Gray

12. Dark Gray

13. Light Green

14. Green

15. Medium Gray

16. Light Gray

17. Sky Blue

1. Black

2. Dark Brown

3. Light Orange

4. Light Brown

5. Light Brown

6. Dark Orange

7. Dark Yellow

8. Medium Orange

9. Medium Brown

10. Brown

11. Gray

12. Light Gray

13. Dark Gray

14. Dark Green

15. Green

16. Light Green

17. Sky Blue

1. Black

2. Dark Brown

3. Light Orange

4. Light Yellow

5. Yellow

6. Orange

7. Beige

8. Light Brown

9. Medium Orange

10. Dark Yellow

11. Brown

12. Medium Brown

13. Dark Red

14. Army Green

15. Light Green

16. Green

17. Dark Green

18. Sky Blue

1. Black

2. Dark Brown

3. Light Orange

4. Medium Orange

5. Light Brown

6. Beige

7. Brown

8. Dark Green

9. Green

10. Medium Green

11. Army Green

12. Neon Green

13. Yellow

14. Light Blue

15. Light Pink

16. Violet

17. Light Violet

18. Red

1. Black

2. Dark Brown

3. Medium Brown

4. Yellow

5. Orange

6. Medium Orange

7. Light Yellow

8. Light Brown

9. Light Orange

10. Beige

11. Dark Yellow

12. Medium Yellow

13. Blue

14. Light Pink

15. Violet

16. Sky Blue

17. Light Violet

1. Black

2. Dark Brown

3. Light Yellow

4. Light Orange

5. Yellow

6. Orange

7. Beige

8. Light Brown

9. Dark Yellow

10. Brown

11. Light Gray

12. Gray

13. Dark Gray

14. Light Green

15. Green

16. Dark Red

17. Medium Brown

18. Sky Blue

ENJOY BONUS
IMAGES FROM SOME
OF OUR
OTHER FUN
COLOR BY NUMBER
BOOKS!

FIND ALL OF OUR
BOOKS
ON AMAZON

Easy Design
Adult Color By Number
Jumbo Coloring Book of Large Print
Flowers, Birds, and Butterflies

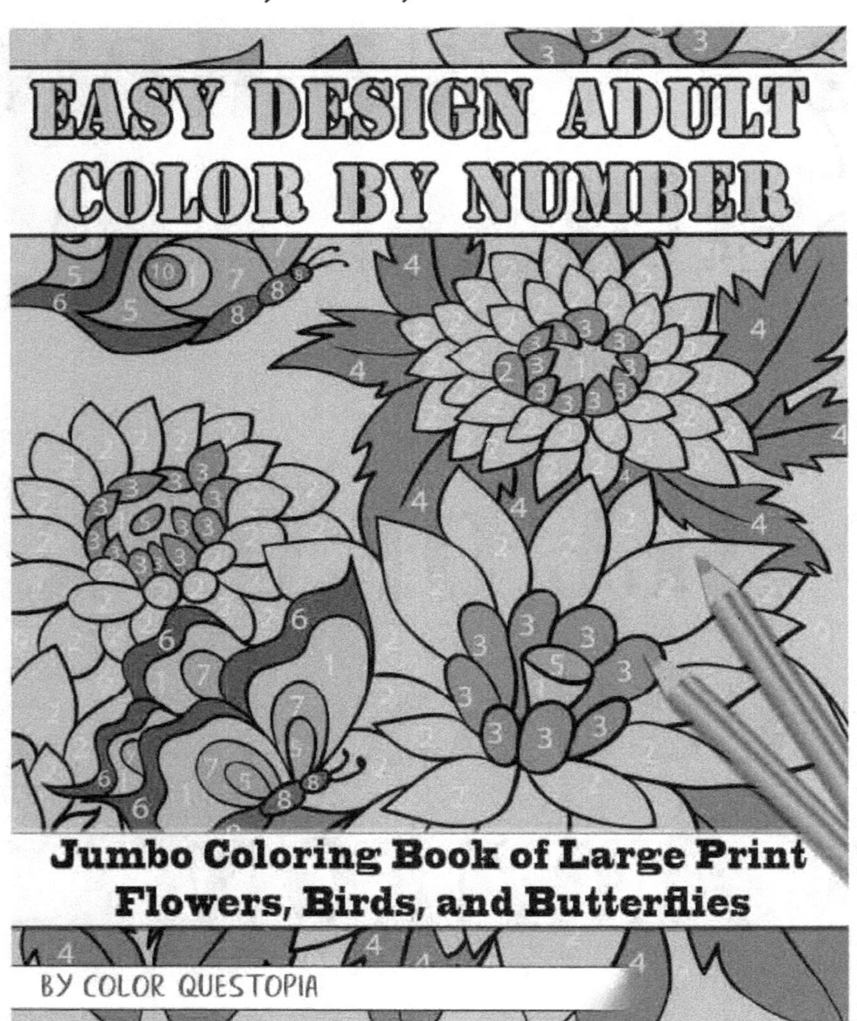

1. Pink   2. Yellow   3. Orange   4. Light Green   5.Sky Blue   6. Blue
7. Purple   8. Brown   9. Green   10. Light Pink   11. Light Violet

Horses Jumbo Adult Coloring Book
Horses and Ponies Grazing and Racing
Color by Number

1. Dark brown

2. Dark Orange

3. Brown

4. Red

5. Medium Brown

6. Dark Orange

7. Orange

8. White

9. Light brown

10. Light Gray

11. Light Orange

12. Dark Yellow

13. Black

14. Army green

15. Light Red

16. Dark Red

17. Sky blue

18. Blue

19. Dark blue

20. Light blue

Amazing Owls
Mosaic Color by Number
Adult Coloring Book for Stress Relief
and Relaxation

1. Black

2. Blue

3. Dark Orange

4. Light Brown

5. Orange

6. Medium Orange

7. Light Orange

8. Yellow

9. Light Yellow

10. Medium Brown

11. Brown

12. Dark Brown

13. Light Green

14. Green

15. Neon Green

16. Light Blue

17. Medium Blue

New York
Mosaic Color by Number
Coloring Book for Adults

1. Yellow

2. Light Yellow

3. Brown

4. Medium Brown

5. Light Brown

6. Light Orange

7. Violet

8. Dark Violet

9. Red

10. Dark Gray

11. Light Gray

12. Gray

13. Medium Gray

14. Gray Purple

15. Dark Brown

16. White

17. Sky Blue

Country Farm Scenes
Nature, Animal, and Easy Designs
Adult Coloring Book
Color By Number For Adults

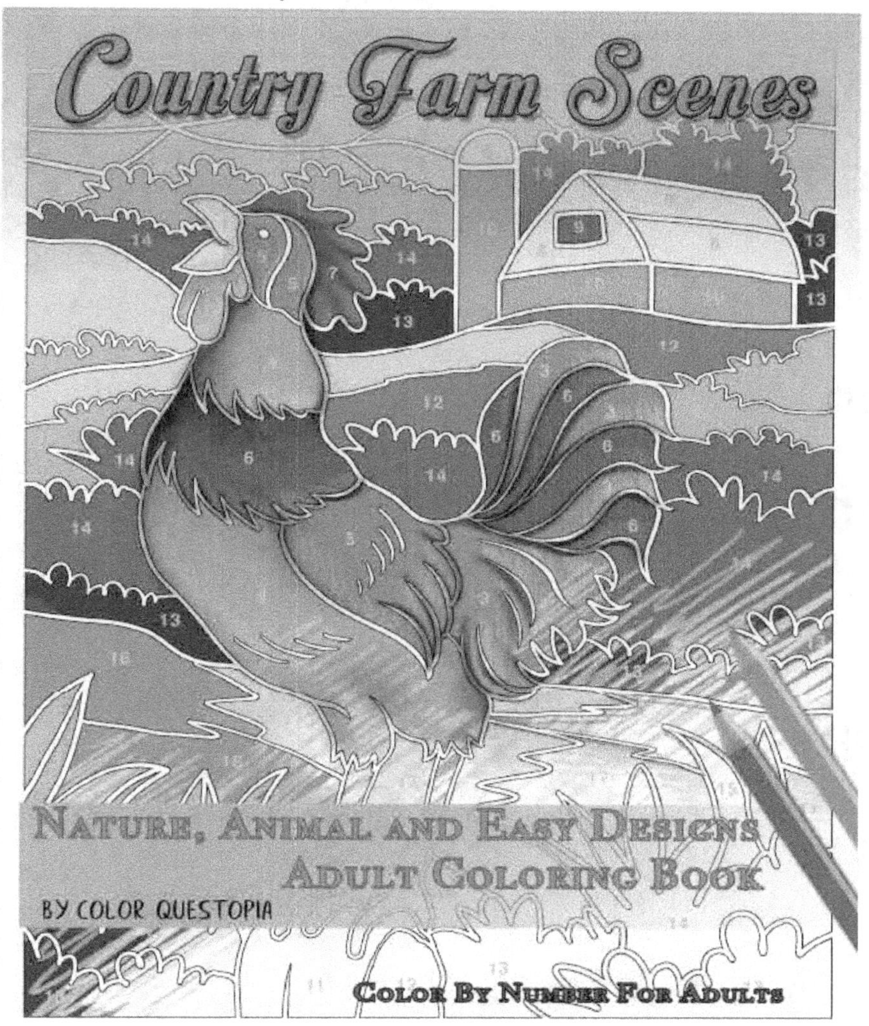

1. Dark Brown

2. Yellow

3. Orange

4. Light Orange

5. Light Red

6. Red

7. Brown

8. Dark Green

9. Green

10. Neon Green

11. Light Green

12. Green

13. Army Green

14. Light Brown

15. Light Yellow

16. Blue

17. Light Blue

Please
Leave
Us
A Review
On Amazon